W9-AHJ-419

Elsmere Library
30 Spruce Avenue
Wilmington, DE 19805

Savvy

Custom Confections

SUGARCOAT IT!

DESSERTS TO DESIGN, DECORATE, AND DEVOUR

by Jen Besel

CAPSTONE PRESS

a capstone imprint

Savvy Books are published by Capstone Press,
1710 Roe Crest Drive, North Mankato, Minnesota 56003
www.capstonepub.com

Library of Congress Cataloging-in-Publication Data
Besel, Jennifer M., author.
Sugarcoat it!: desserts to design, decorate, and devour / by Jen Besel.
pages cm. – (Savvy. Custom confections.)
Summary: "Step-by-step instructions teach readers how to decorate delicious desserts,
including cakes, cupcakes, cookies, and more" – Provided by publisher.
Audience: Age 9-13.
Audience: Grade 4 to 6.
Includes bibliographical references and index.
ISBN 978-1-4914-0861-2 (library binding)
1. Cake decorating—Juvenile literature. I. Title. II. Title: Sugar coat it!
TX771.2.B465 2015
641.86'539–dc23   2014001838

Editorial Credits
Ashlee Suker, designer; Sarah Schuette, photo stylist; Marcy Morin, scheduler;
Danielle Ceminsky, production specialist

Photo Credits
All images by Capstone Studio: Karon Dubke

Printed in the United States of America in North Mankato, Minnesota.
032014   008087CGF14

TABLE of CONTENTS

STUNNING DESSERTS

... Decorated by You!

Clear off the counter. Grab your tools. And get ready!
You're about to decorate treats that look as good as
they taste. Want to really jazz up that store-bought treat?
Need an elegant cake for that special event? Or do you
just want to serve something unexpected? You've come to
the right place.

You don't need to be a professional baker to make custom
desserts. With a few ingredients and some simple steps, you
can create your own beautiful masterpieces. And you won't
have to spend days in the kitchen to do it. (But you can let
your guests think you did.)

So jump right in. What custom
confection will you decorate first?

Convert It

The recipes in this book use U. S. measurements.
If you need metric measurements, here's a
handy conversion guide.

United States	Metric
¼ teaspoon	1.2 mL
½ teaspoon	2.5 mL
1 teaspoon	5 mL
1 tablespoon	15 mL
¼ cup	60 mL
⅓ cup	80 mL
½ cup	120 mL
⅔ cup	160 mL
¾ cup	175 mL
1 cup	240 mL
1 quart	1 liter
1 ounce	30 grams
2 ounces	55 grams
4 ounces	110 grams
½ pound	225 grams
1 pound	455 grams

TOOLS

You'll need some kitchen tools to create mouthwatering treats. But don't worry. You probably have most of these in your kitchen already.

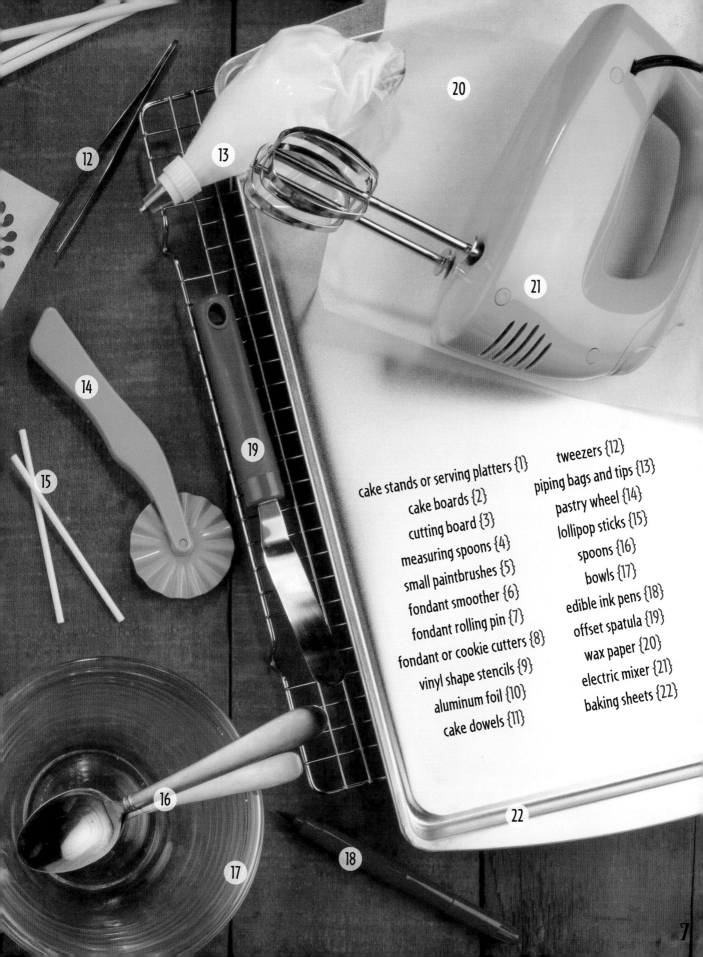

cake stands or serving platters {1}
cake boards {2}
cutting board {3}
measuring spoons {4}
small paintbrushes {5}
fondant smoother {6}
fondant rolling pin {7}
fondant or cookie cutters {8}
vinyl shape stencils {9}
aluminum foil {10}
cake dowels {11}

tweezers {12}
piping bags and tips {13}
pastry wheel {14}
lollipop sticks {15}
spoons {16}
bowls {17}
edible ink pens {18}
offset spatula {19}
wax paper {20}
electric mixer {21}
baking sheets {22}

2 tablespoons water

2 tablespoons powdered egg white

fresh edible flowers, such as violets or impatiens, with stems removed

¼ cup granulated sugar

flood royal icing *(See page 45 for recipe.)*

food coloring, if desired

cupcakes, any flavor

Edible Flowers

Don't use flowers from your backyard for any desserts. They could have poisonous pesticides on them. Go to a flower shop, and ask the florist for pesticide-free edible flowers.

SUGARED FLOWER
Cupcakes

Go from plain cupcake to stunning confection
with just a little icing and a flower on top.

1 Cover a baking sheet with wax paper and set aside.

2 Combine the water and powdered egg white
in a small bowl. Beat together with a fork.

3 Use a small paintbrush to cover a flower with
egg white mixture.

4 Hold the flower over an empty bowl. Sprinkle sugar over the
flower. Lay the flower on a baking sheet.

5 Repeat steps 3–4 with the other flowers. Let the
flowers dry overnight.

6 If desired, add a few drops of food coloring to the royal
icing and stir. Then pour the icing into a piping bag or
small squeeze bottle.

7 Pipe icing over the top of one cupcake, starting in the center
and moving out in a circular motion. Gently shake the cupcake
to spread the icing into a smooth layer.

8 Arrange sugared flowers on top of the icing while it's
still wet.

9 Repeat steps 7 and 8 with all the cupcakes. Let the icing
dry for at least one hour.

PAINTED *Cookies*

Add a splash of color to store-bought cookies with homemade gel. Put a little edible glitter in the gel, and your dessert will really sparkle.

½ cup cold water

2 tablespoons cornstarch

½ cup corn syrup

1 teaspoon clear vanilla

gel food coloring

edible glitter

light-colored cookies with smooth tops, such as lemon wafer cookies

1 Mix the water and cornstarch together in a small microwavable bowl.

2 Stir in the corn syrup and vanilla.

3 Microwave the mixture on high for one minute, 30 seconds or until the mixture boils and turns clear.

4 Set the bowl on your work surface to cool. Whisk the mixture every couple of minutes.

5 When the mixture is at room temperature, mix in food coloring to create the color you want. Add 1 or 2 teaspoons of edible glitter to the mixture.

6 Pour the colored gel into a small squeeze bottle. Squeeze the gel onto the cookies in any shape or design you want. You could even write names or initials on the cookies.

7 When you're done, put the cookies on wax paper to set for at least one hour.

CREAM PUFF *Tree*

Let dessert be the centerpiece of your next gathering. Everyone will crowd around the table for this deliciously beautiful display.

about 100 frozen cream puffs, thawed

caramel syrup

chocolate syrup

¼ cup white chocolate chips

red gumdrops

1 Carefully wrap an 8-inch foam cone with aluminum foil. Then place the cone on a serving plate.

2 Cover three baking sheets with wax paper. Divide the cream puffs into three groups and put them on the baking sheets.

3 Drizzle caramel syrup over the cream puffs on one baking sheet. Then drizzle chocolate syrup over the cream puffs on another baking sheet.

4 Put the white chocolate chips in a microwave-safe bowl. Heat for 30 seconds on the defrost setting. Stir. Heat again until the chips are melted and smooth when you stir them. Drizzle the melted white chocolate over the puffs on the third baking sheet.

5 Let the puffs sit in the refrigerator for about 30 minutes.

6 Stick a toothpick into one cream puff. Then attach the cream puff to the foam cone. Continue adding cream puffs around the bottom of the cone, alternating the chocolate, caramel, and white chocolate ones. Put the puffs as close together as you can.

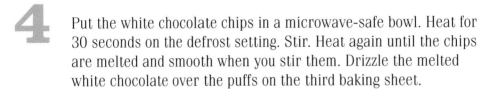

7 Put a gumdrop on one end of a toothpick. Then attach it to the cone just above and between two puffs. Continue sticking in gumdrops around the cone between the puffs.

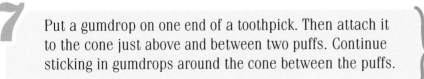

8 Continue placing cream puffs and gumdrops around the cone. The puffs should stack directly on top of each other. The gumdrops should fill the spaces between the puffs. Top off the tree with a trio of puffs.

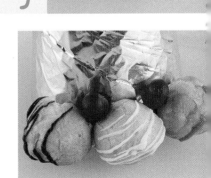

vanilla buttercream
frosting *(See page 46
for recipe.)*

food coloring

chocolate buttercream
frosting *(See page 46
for recipe.)*

5 cupcakes, any flavor

sprinkles

mini chocolate chips

1 sugar cone

maraschino cherry

ICE CREAM CONE
Cupcakes

Have everyone screaming for ice cream with this fun spin on cupcakes.

1. Divide the vanilla buttercream frosting into bowls.

2. Add food coloring to all but one of the bowls and stir well. Leave one bowl white.

3. Put each color of frosting, including the chocolate, into a separate zip-top bag and close tightly. For each bag, press the frosting down into one corner, and snip off the tip of the bag.

4. Pipe one color of frosting onto a cupcake with a swirling motion. After the top of the cupcake is covered, add extra swirls of frosting to one edge to make the cupcake look like a scoop of ice cream.

5. Garnish the frosted cupcake with sprinkles, chocolate chips, or whatever candies you like.

6. Repeat steps 4 and 5 with the rest of the cupcakes, using the colors of frosting as you wish.

7. Arrange the cupcakes on a serving platter so they look like they are sitting on top of each other.

8. Spread chocolate frosting around the top edge of the cone. Then press sprinkles into the frosting.

9. Lay the cone under the bottom cupcake. Gently press the cone into the cupcake so it looks as if the cupcake is in the cone.

10. Finish the arrangement with a cherry on top.

SIMPLY STENCILED
Cake

Take cake from drab to fab with just a stencil and frosting. Go wild and crazy or fun and frilly. It's all up to you!

Cake Stencils

Any clean vinyl stencils can be used to decorate a cake. Look for stencils in your local hobby supply store. You'll want small designs for the sides and a large design for the top.

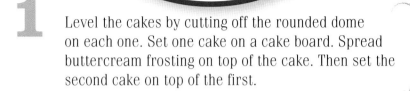

2 9-inch round cakes, any flavor

vanilla buttercream frosting *(See page 46 for recipe.)*

food coloring

marshmallow fondant, colored as you wish *(See page 44 for recipe.)*

powdered sugar

sugar pearls

1 Level the cakes by cutting off the rounded dome on each one. Set one cake on a cake board. Spread buttercream frosting on top of the cake. Then set the second cake on top of the first.

2 Spread a thin layer of frosting over the sides and top of the stacked cake.

3 Generously sprinkle powdered sugar over your work surface. Use a rolling pin to press the fondant into an 18-inch circle. Roll the fondant onto the pin, and then gently lay it over the stacked cake.

4 Smooth any wrinkles in the fondant. Then trim away excess at the bottom.

5 Color the buttercream frosting as you wish.

6 Carefully hold a small vinyl stencil against the side of the cake. Have a partner help you hold it in place. Carefully spread buttercream over the stencil. When you've filled in all the spaces, carefully pull the stencil straight off the cake.

7 Wipe off the stencil, then reposition it on the side of the cake, aligning it with where you left off. Spread frosting over the stencil again. Continue all around the cake.

8 Place a large stencil on top of the cake. Spread buttercream as you did on the sides. Lift the stencil straight up when you're done.

9 Carefully place sugar pearls in the buttercream.

TIERED FONDANT *Cake*

Build up layers of deliciousness with this classic tiered cake. Using a sweet marshmallow fondant, you can make your cake and eat it too.

2 10-inch square cakes, any flavor

vanilla buttercream frosting
(See page 46 for recipe.)

2 6-inch square cakes, any flavor

powdered sugar

uncolored marshmallow fondant
(See page 44 for recipe.)

1 Trace a 6-inch square cake board on a piece of scratch paper, and cut it out. Set the paper square aside.

2 Put one 10-inch cake on a 10-inch square cake board. Spread a layer of vanilla buttercream frosting on the top. Lay the second 10-inch cake on top.

3 Repeat step 2 with the 6-inch cakes and a 6-inch cake board.

4 Frost the tops and sides of the layered 10-inch cake with vanilla buttercream.

5 Generously dust your work surface with powdered sugar. Roll the fondant out into a large square. It doesn't have to be perfect. You just want to make sure you have it large enough to cover your cake.

6 Lay the rolling pin along the bottom edge of your fondant square. Curl the edge of the fondant around the pin, and roll the fondant onto it.

7 Unroll the fondant over the 10-inch cake.

continued on next page

8 Gently smooth the fondant on the top of the cake using a circular motion. You can use a fondant smoother or your hands.

9 Smooth the sides of the cake.

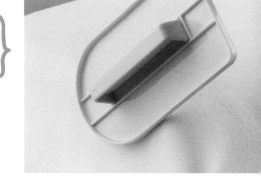

10 Cut off any extra fondant at the bottom of the cake.

11 Repeat steps 4–10 with the layered 6-inch cake.

12 Center the paper square on top of the 10-inch cake. Gently trace around the paper with a toothpick. Remove the paper square.

13 Gently push a cake dowel all the way into the cake at one corner of the traced square. Mark the height of the cake on the dowel with a pencil. Remove the dowel and cut at the line. Cut four more dowel pieces the same height.

14 Press four dowels into the cake at the four corners of the traced square. Press one into the center.

15 Carefully place the 6-inch cake and cake board on top of the 10-inch cake along the dowel lines.

16 Wrap ribbon around the bottom of the 6-inch cake, covering the cake board. Attach the ribbon to the cake with a dab of vanilla buttercream.

17 Repeat step 16 on the bottom cake.

18 If you wish, arrange pesticide-free flowers on the cake tiers. Attach each flower with a dab of buttercream.

ROYALLY ICED Cookies

Ever wonder how they get those gorgeous designs on cookies? Well, the secret is out! With royal icing, toothpicks, and a little practice, you'll be decorating your own eye-catching cookies in no time.

1

Divide the edge royal icing into bowls. Color each bowl of icing as desired. Divide and color the flood icing just as you did with edge icing. Pour each icing into a separate piping bag.

edge and flood royal icing
(See page 45 for recipe.)

food coloring

sugar cookies

2

To create hearts, pipe edge royal icing around the outside edge of a cookie. Then fill in the shape with flood icing of the same color. While the icing is still wet, pipe small dots of flood icing of a different color on the cookie. Drag a toothpick through the center of each dot to make a heart.

3

To create chevrons, pipe edge royal icing around the outside edge of a cookie. Then fill in the shape with flood royal icing of the same color. While the icing is still wet, pipe straight lines of other colors of flood icing across the cookie. Starting at the top of the cookie, drag a toothpick through the lines. Repeat as many times as you wish, always starting at the top.

4

To create starbursts, pipe edge royal icing around the outside edge of the cookie. Then fill in the shape with flood royal icing of the same color. While the icing is still wet, pipe circles on the cookie, one inside the next. Starting in the center of the cookie, drag a toothpick in a straight line through the circles. Go back to the center and repeat in different spots around the cookie.

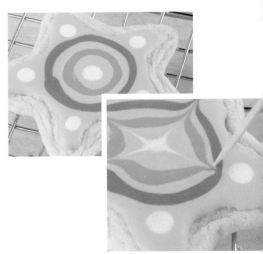

FARM FRIENDS
Cake Pops

Turn cake balls into adorable farmyard animals. Your friends will squeal with delight.

1. Crumble the cake into a bowl so there are no large pieces.

2. Add a spoonful of frosting to the crumbled cake. Mix well. Continue adding spoonfuls of frosting and mixing until the mixture is a moist dough that you can mold into balls. You'll probably use most of a tub of frosting.

3. Cover a baking sheet with wax paper. Roll the cake dough into 2-inch balls. Arrange on the baking sheet.

4. Melt a small amount of white melting wafers according to package directions.

5. Dip one end of a lollipop stick into the melted candy. Then press the coated stick end into a cake ball. Repeat with all the balls.

6. Place the cake balls with sticks into the freezer for about 20 minutes. Then let them come to room temperature before moving to the next step.

7. To make a cow, dip a cake ball into melted white candy. Place a red mini candy-coated candy on as a nose. Use two mini chocolate chips for horns. Press the lollipop stick into a block of foam, and let the candy dry for at least 30 minutes. Use a small paintbrush to apply melted chocolate wafers as spots. Use a black edible-ink pen to draw eyes and nostrils. Let the candy dry again.

8. To make a pig, cut a pink round candy in half. Dip a cake pop in melted pink candy wafers. Put the candy halves on as ears. Use a full pink round candy for a nose. Let dry. Then use a black edible-ink pen to draw on eyes, mouth, and nostrils.

9. To make a chick, dip a cake pop in melted yellow candy wafers. Press orange candy hearts into the ball to look like a beak. Press on flower pastels for feet. Also press in small white candy hearts along the top of the cake pop. Let dry. Use a black edible-ink pen to draw eyes.

1 9x13-inch cake or
2 9-inch round cakes,
any flavor

1 tub of frosting, any flavor

white, pink, chocolate,
and yellow candy
melting wafers

red mini
candy-coated candies

mini chocolate chips

black edible-ink pen

pink round candies

orange and white
candy hearts

orange flower-shaped
pastels

EDIBLE Decorations

Prepare to be amazed with this surprising dessert decoration. With just gelatin, water, and a paintbrush, you can create edible bows and butterflies to top any creation.

To Make the Gelatin

1 Put the water into a small microwaveable bowl. Stir in food coloring to your desired color.

2 Add gelatin to the water. Stir until there are no clumps.

3 Microwave the mixture for 20 seconds. Then let the mixture sit for about 10 minutes.

4 Use a spoon to scrape away the layer of foam that settles on top of the gelatin.

5 Reheat the bowl of gelatin for about 10 seconds or just until it's a warm liquid. It's now ready to use to create decorations.

6 tablespoons water

gel food coloring

1 tablespoon unflavored gelatin

edible glitter, optional

continued on next page

Making Gelatin Shapes

1 Use a paintbrush to brush the warm liquid gelatin into the cavities of a gelatin mold. Make sure you cover the entire surface, but don't leave liquid puddling inside.

2 If desired, sprinkle the wet gelatin with edible glitter.

3 Let the gelatin set for about one hour.

4 Gently pop the gelatin shapes out of the mold. Trim away any excess gelatin, if necessary.

5 Press the gelatin shapes into freshly frosted cupcakes. Or pipe a bit of extra frosting onto a frosted cake and press the shapes into it.

Making Gelatin Bows

1 Use a paintbrush to paint the entire surface of a flexible chopping mat with liquid gelatin. Go over the mat three or four times to get a good coverage. Set the leftover gelatin aside. Let the gelatin set for about one hour. As it hardens, the gelatin might curl up a bit.

2 Lift the dry gelatin paper off the mat. Cut it into 1-inch wide strips. Then cut each strip in half lengthwise.

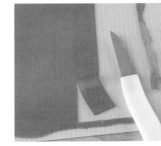

3 Reheat the bowl of gelatin for about 10 seconds or just until it's a warm liquid.

4 Paint one end of a gelatin strip with a bit of warm liquid gelatin. Fold the strip over to make a loop, pressing the ends together until they are stuck. Repeat with 15 more strips.

5 Arrange six loops in a circle with the ends pointing toward the middle. Glue the loops together by painting them with a bit of liquid gelatin and pressing until they stick. Use a long lollipop stick to help you pick up and press the loops.

6 Add more loops to the center of the circle, offsetting the loops as you build up the bow. Paint on liquid gelatin as glue to stick the loops to each other. You'll finish by adding a loop standing up in the middle.

7 Pipe a bit of frosting onto a frosted cake where you want the bow. Press the bow into the frosting.

DUNKED & DIPPED *Treats*

This is one of the easiest and most entertaining desserts around. Dip and dunk all kinds of treats–from pretzels to strawberries. Get your friends together and have fun dunking your treats together.

1 Pour sprinkles and nuts into separate small bowls.

2 Melt the chocolate and white chocolate melting wafers according to package directions.

3 While the chocolates are still warm, dip a treat into one flavor of chocolate about half way.

4 Pour sprinkles or nuts over the treat, if you want.

5 If desired, drizzle the treat with the opposite color of melted chocolate.

6 Lay the treat on wax paper or stand it up in a jar. Let it rest until the chocolate has dried.

7 Mix and match chocolates and toppings on the other cookies, pretzels, and strawberries. You could even experiment with dipping different kinds of cookies or fruit.

sprinkles

chopped nuts

chocolate melting wafers

white chocolate melting wafers

pretzel rods

biscotti cookies

chocolate chip cookies

strawberries, washed and patted dry

Big-Eyed Owl Cake

Decorate your way to hoots of happiness. A simple smeared dot technique gives this bird its feathers.

1 10-inch round cake, any flavor

chocolate buttercream frosting
(*See page 46 for recipe.*)

2 6-inch round cakes, any flavor
food coloring

vanilla buttercream frosting
(*See page 46 for recipe.*)

2 chocolate-covered cookies

2 red candy-coated candies

1 Put the 10-inch cake on your work surface. Lay a 6-inch round cake pan on the edge of the cake so it overlaps about 2 inches. Cut along the pan edge to remove an oval from the large cake. Then move the pan over and repeat the cut so you have two oval cutouts.

2 Lay the cake pan on the edge of the 10-inch cake directly below the oval cutouts, again overlapping about 2 inches. Cut out an arch shape from the cake.

3 Place the cut 10-inch cake on an 18-inch round cake board. Spread chocolate buttercream frosting along the two cut edges at the top of the cake. Nestle the 6-inch cakes into the cuts. It should look like a body with two large eyes.

4 Cut one of the oval pieces from step 1 in half widthwise. Spread chocolate frosting on the sides of the pieces. Place them just above the eyes. Then place the arch-shaped piece of cake you removed in step 2 above the eyes to finish the head.

5 Spread chocolate frosting over the owl's wings, between the eyes, and on the head. Leave the eyes and the center of the body unfrosted.

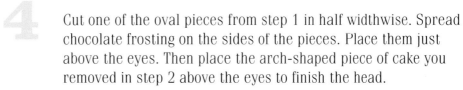

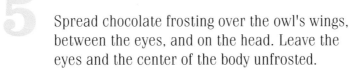

continued on next page **33**

6 Color some vanilla buttercream orange. Put it in a piping bag with a round tip. Then fit another piping bag with a large round tip. Fill this bag with uncolored vanilla buttercream.

7 Pipe a row of round white frosting drops on the bottom of the body. Add a bead of orange frosting on top of each white drop. Use a spatula to flatten the frosting drops, then pull them up toward the eyes. Continue adding rows of frosting drops and pulling them up until the body is covered in frosting feathers.

8 Use orange buttercream to frost the eyes. Then add drops of more orange frosting around the edges of the eyes. Use a spatula to flatten the frosting drops and pull them toward the center.

9 Set a chocolate-covered cookie in the center of each eye. Pipe a small white dot on each cookie and top with a red candy-coated candy.

10 Color a small amount of vanilla buttercream yellow. Put it in a piping bag with a round tip.

11 Pipe a triangle of yellow frosting between the eyes as a beak. Then pipe feet on the cake edge between the wings.

MONSTER Brownies

Take brownies to the wild side with a drizzle of frosting and some creepy eyes. They're the perfect mix of sweet and scary.

a pan of brownies

vanilla buttercream frosting
(See page 46 for recipe.)

food coloring

gummy rings

mini chocolate chips

mini marshmallows

mini candy-coated candies

1 Cut the brownies into squares, and remove them from the pan.

2 Separate the buttercream frosting into bowls. Color each bowl of frosting a different "monster-ific" color. Put each color into a separate zip-top bag. Squeeze the frosting down to one corner, and cut off the tip.

3 Pipe long, stringy lines of frosting across one brownie. Start each line in the center and work toward the edge, letting the frosting hang over the sides.

4 Make eyes by putting two gummy rings on top of the frosted brownie. Press chocolate chips into the holes in the rings.

5 Pipe another color of frosting on another brownie using the same technique as in step 3.

6 Make different eyes by setting marshmallows in the frosting. Put a dab of frosting on each marshmallow. Then stick a mini candy-coated candy on each dab of frosting.

7 Continue frosting the brownies and making eyes. Give some of your monsters one eye, and give others three eyes.

4 9x13-inch cakes,
any flavor

food coloring

vanilla buttercream frosting
(See page 46 for recipe.)

marshmallow fondant,
colored as you wish
(See page 44 for recipe.)

TASTY TREATS

DELICIOUS

CAKE 101

PILE-OF-BOOKS Cake

Love a good book and a good dessert? Bring these two loves together with this pile-of-books cake. These are the kinds of books you can really sink your teeth into.

1. Cut a piece of cardboard so it's 9x11 inches. Cut two 8x10-inch pieces. Then cut one piece that's 4½x6½ inches. Cover each cardboard piece with aluminum foil. These will be your cake boards.

2. Level the top of each cake. Also trim off any crusty edges so you have four neat rectangular cakes.

3. Cut 2 inches off a short side of one cake to make a 9x11-inch cake.

4. Cut 3 inches off a short side of another cake. Then trim off 1 inch from one long side. Then cut the cake in half horizontally, so you end up with two thin 8x10-inch cakes.

5. Cut a third cake in half so you have two 4½x6½-inch cakes.

6. Place the fourth 9x13-inch cake on a large wooden cutting board or large serving plate.

7. Color some buttercream as you wish. Spread the frosting over the top and one long edge of the cake.

8. Spread white frosting on the other three sides of the cake. While the frosting is still wet, drag the tines of a fork gently through the white frosting to make it look like pages.

~continued on next page~

9 Gently drag a thin spatula or the handle of a wooden spoon through the frosting along the colored long edge. This should look like where the book's cover would bend.

10 Place the 9x11-inch cake and the two 8x10-inch cakes on the cake boards of the same sizes. Then repeat steps 7–9 with each cake.

11 Put one of the 4½x6½-inch cakes on the same size cake board. Spread buttercream frosting on top. Then set the second cake on top. Frost this thick cake as you've done the others. You should now have five separate books.

12 Press dowels into the 9x13-inch cake where the corners of the 9x11-inch cake will sit. Also press one into the middle. Trim the dowels so they don't stand taller than the top of the cake.

13 Gently stack the 9x11-inch cake on top of the first cake over the dowels.

14 Repeat steps 12–13 to stack the rest of the cakes. Then pipe frosting along the bottom edges of each book to make it look as if there's a bottom cover.

15 Generously dust your work surface with powdered sugar. Roll out the fondant. Use alphabet-shaped cutters to punch out letters to add titles to the books. Also cut out decorations, such as diamonds for the spines, if you wish.

16 Let the letters and decorations dry for about one hour. Pipe a bit of buttercream onto the back of each fondant letter or decoration, and stick them onto the cake.

HEDGEHOG *Cake*

Go for the unexpected with this wacky hedgehog cake. With slivered almonds for spines and a marshmallow treat head, this cake will be a delicious surprise.

2 6-inch round cakes, any flavor

vanilla buttercream frosting
(See page 46 for recipe.)

crispy rice marshmallow treats

chocolate buttercream frosting
(See page 46 for recipe.)

1 round vanilla wafer cookie

3 brown candy-coated candies

slivered almonds

1 Lay a round cake on your work surface. Spread vanilla buttercream on top. Lay the second cake on top of the first.

2 Cut two sides of the layered cake off so you have two straight edges and two rounded edges. Stand the cake up on one straight edge.

3 Sculpt marshmallow treats into a head with a pointed snout. The head should be as tall as the cake stack and fit nicely against the straight edge. You can heat the treats in the microwave for about 15 seconds to make them easier to mold.

4 Put the body and head on a serving platter. Spread vanilla buttercream frosting over the face and the body.

5 Spread a thin layer of chocolate frosting over the snout. Use a fork to draw lines on the face to look like fur.

6 Cut a vanilla wafer in half. Press the halves into the cake just behind the face to make ears. Then add candy-coated candies as eyes and a nose.

7 Dip a slivered almond about half way into chocolate frosting. Then press the chocolate-covered end into the cake body. Continue dipping and pressing the almonds in until the entire body is covered in almond spines.

Marshmallow Fondant

4 cups plus some extra powdered sugar
8 ounces mini marshmallows
4 tablespoons water
food coloring, if desired
shortening

1. Generously dust your work surface with powdered sugar.

2. Put the marshmallows and water in a large microwave-safe bowl. Heat on high for one minute.

3. Stir the marshmallows until they are smooth.

4. If you want to color the fondant, add food coloring to the marshmallow mixture and stir.

5. Pour four cups of powdered sugar into the bowl. Stir until the mixture becomes too stiff to stir anymore.

6. Dump the sugar mixture onto your prepared work surface.

7. Coat your hands with shortening, then knead the sugar mixture. Continue kneading until the mixture becomes smooth. If the fondant starts sticking to your hands, put more shortening on them.

8. Once it's smooth, the fondant is ready to be rolled out and put on your cake.

Royal Icing

2 teaspoons meringue powder
2 tablespoons water
2 to 2½ cups powdered sugar

Edge and flood royal icings are made with the same ingredients.
The only difference is how stiff you make the icing. Stiffer edge
icing is perfect for creating outlines or decorations that need to
hold a shape. Use flood icing to easily cover a large area.

Edge Icing

With an electric mixer on high, blend the ingredients together
in a bowl for about four to five minutes. The icing is the right
consistency when it forms little peaks that hold their shape. Pour
the edge icing into a piping bag with a round tip to create designs
or borders.

Flood Icing

Make a batch of edge icing. Then add water ½ teaspoon at a time,
blending after each addition. The icing is ready when drips hold
their shape for just a moment before they blend back into the
icing. Spoon this icing onto a cookie or other dessert. Then use a
toothpick or small paintbrush to spread it out.

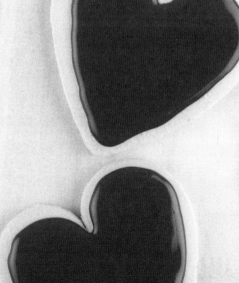

Vanilla Buttercream Frosting

½ cup unsalted butter,
softened

½ teaspoon vanilla extract

2 cups powdered sugar

1-2 tablespoons milk

1. In a large bowl, cream the butter and vanilla until fluffy.

2. Alternate adding sugar and milk until the ingredients are mixed well. The frosting should be thick, creamy, and spreadable. Scrape the sides of the bowl often with a spatula.

Variations

For chocolate frosting, follow the recipe above, and add ¼ cup unsweetened cocoa powder along with the sugar.

For peanut butter frosting, follow the recipe above but leave out the vanilla extract. Add in 1 cup creamy peanut butter and an extra tablespoon of milk.

For cherry frosting, replace the milk with maraschino cherry juice. Replace the vanilla with almond extract.

Piping Tips

To make a rose:

1. Put a 1mm open star tip on the piping bag. Hold the bag straight up from a cake top. Squeeze out a star.

2. Continue squeezing with even pressure, and swirl frosting around the star without lifting the bag up. When the top is covered, stop squeezing and pull the bag straight away from the cake.

To make a cupcake swirl:

1. Put a 1mm open star tip on the piping bag. Hold the bag straight up from a cake top. Squeeze out a star.

2. Continue squeezing with even pressure while lifting the bag slightly. Swirl frosting around the cake until the top is covered.

3. Continue squeezing as you move back to the center of the cupcake. Do another swirl on top of the first. Then stop squeezing and pull the bag straight away from the cupcake.

Glossary

DRIZZLE (DRIZ-uhl)—to let a substance fall in small drops

EDIBLE (ED-uh-buhl)—able to be eaten

FONDANT (FAWN-dent)—a soft, creamy icing that can be rolled out like dough

GARNISH (GAR-nish)—something added to a dish for flavor or decoration

LEVEL (LE-val)—to make flat

Read More

Besel, Jen. *Sweet Tooth!: No-Bake Desserts to Make and Devour.* Custom Confections. North Mankato, Minn.: Capstone Press, 2015.

Rau, Dana Meachen. *Piece of Cake! Decorating Awesome Cakes.* Dessert Designer. North Mankato, Minn.: Capstone Press, 2013.

Tack, Karen. *Hello, Cupcake! What's New?* Boston: Houghton Mifflin Harcourt, 2011.

Internet Sites

FactHound offers a safe, fun way to find Internet sites related to this book. All of the sites on FactHound have been researched by our staff.

Here's all you do:

Visit *www.facthound.com*

Type in this code: 9781491408612